A Gift For My Mother

This gift is for

_____

A Gift For My Mother

By Keisha. A Toby
Edited By Latoya Toby Thomas

Dedication

This book is dedicated to my son, Kelechi, who gave this gift to me at the age of six,

and who reminds me every day to live and love and never give up.

To all the children I have had the pleasure of working with.

To my family and friends who stood with me when times got hard

It is also dedicated to all the single mothers and struggling parents.

Always remember that your starting place is not your finishing place.

Never let your current situation dictate your future.

Special Thanks to

Pastor Basil Miller and all my friends at Scarborough Church of God for Godly inspiration.

Thanks to all the teachers and mentors I have met along this journey.

Thanks to Sherri Gilbert who reminded me to always share my stories.

Jeffrey Canton from York University Children Studies as we read many children's

books, opened my eyes to the discourses that were not told.

Thanks to all the children I shared my stories with, who listened and loved them.

Life is a journey, and we must move forward one step at a time.

Don't give up no matter how difficult it gets.

Stand strong, stay focused and don't give up on your dreams.

Love and appreciation

Keisha Toby

Mom would sit at the kitchen table as she always did, going through her paperwork with such a worried look on her face.

I was only seven years old, but I knew, I understood everything that was happening around me. My Mom thought that because I was little, "a small boy" as she would sometimes call me, She thought I didn't know much.

I would sit across from her at the kitchen table and watch her as she silently worried about everything. How was she going to take care of all the bills and how was she going to take care of me? She never told me, but I knew we had little.

This small boy understood that all those letters in the mail were bills. I knew my life was different. Sometimes, only sometimes I just wanted to be like the kids I saw on tv or in the books my mom read to me ending happily ever after. My life was not so.

My mom would always say that having lots of stuff was not important, it does not bring happiness, and it does not add to our lives. Having good health that's what we should be most thankful for, but mom was not a child. It was a long time since she was a child.

She just did not understand that I have friends who have lots of stuff. Why can't I have stuff too? Sometimes it just felt so unfair. I never complained though, but in my head, I felt it. In my head, I dreamt of having fancy toys. Mom did not know what went on in my head, but I had conversations in my head.

When she read to me at bedtime, she would say "Life is not perfect, but we have a good life." Mom would say, "When you grow up, you will understand more; being a mom to you is the best thing ever, and having you as a son makes life perfect."

She would tell me every night that I was the best son ever, as she kissed me good night with our special nose kisses and reminded me to say my prayers, "Always be thankful for what we have." Sometimes I thought, why should I be thankful? But I was obedient and prayed, did what she said. Mom never knew what was going on in my head.

Let me tell you about Saturdays and why I hated Saturdays. Not all Saturdays were bad, just the ones when mom and I did grocery shopping. Those were the Saturdays I hated the most.

Going grocery shopping with mom was never a good thing, having to get just what we needed and nothing else. If that wasn't bad enough, bad I could only get the cereal I wanted only when it was on sale. I didn't have a choice. I had to eat what we bought. We always had to get groceries that were on sale even though I didn't like it. Mom took the weekly flyers to the store and was always looking for the best deal.

Mom always gave me the calculator; my job was to constantly add prices. Each item mom put in the shopping basket, I always had to report after each price was added. Bread $2, Cereal $5.60 and so I did with what little we got.

"We could never go over our budget" Mom reminded me of this all the time " Don't forget the budget. Mom says shopping this way helps us get the best prices for what we needed and made us smart shoppers. She even said it helped me with my math skills. Shopping this way never got me what I wanted.

I hated it!

I hated money!

I hated our small budget!

I hated shopping! and I hate math!

Let me tell you a story. One Saturday while cashing our groceries out, I really wanted my favorite candy. I really wanted it badly. I begged mom please, can I have a candy? I pleaded, I begged!

My begging became louder and louder, mom ignored me and pretended she did not hear my request. I could not control that feeling of want deep inside my belly; I really wanted that candy, any candy at this point would make me feel better.

I started crying "Whaaaaaaa! Whaaaaaaa! Whaaaaaaa!" my crying turned into screaming. It seemed like every eye in the grocery store was looking at me, but I didn't care, and I could not stop myself.

I could tell my mom was upset and embarrassed, but there was nothing I could do to stop myself crying.

A woman who was in the store behind us was staring at me, saw my pain and saw how upset I was and said to me, "If it is ok with your mom, I would get you the candy." Mom looked at me and said it was ok, but by the look on her face, I knew she was unhappy and embarrassed. I knew this was not the end; she was going to call my aunts and tell them about my behavior.

At this point, I couldn't care less about anything. All I wanted was that candy. Thanks to that lady, I got it! I got what I desperately wanted.

Mom said, "You don't understand that there was not enough money to waste on candy and stuff." I understood well, but this time, I really wanted that candy. Don't get me wrong, it's not that I didn't care about our money issues, but sometimes, a boy just wants to be a boy.

Shopping and then pushing your grocery cart on the street is hard. Sometimes, I knew mom was tired, but she always said, "you do what you have to do" and smiled as we walked along the busy streets.

In the summer, it's ok to push the trolley on the sidewalk, talking to mom and smelling the fragrance of the busy city street where we live. There was always something happening here. In the winter, it was not fun at all pushing the cart over snow. I would have to get bundled up and wear my best gloves because I don't want my hands frozen while pushing a grocery cart down Danforth road. One wheel was constantly falling off the cart through the snow and ice. That was not fun at all.

I always asked, "Why can't we get a car?" "Why can't we get a taxi just for today"? She always said, "There wasn't enough money." I knew life was not perfect for us.

14

I hated Money!

There were many things I wanted to do. I wanted to play soccer on a team, but that would cost extra money. Mom said, "play in the park with your friends, that's a team."

I wanted to do karate lessons. I wanted to do swimming lessons like all my friends. I wanted to swim in the park pool like all my friends all by myself in the summer, but mom said, "There was not enough money" It seemed like there was never enough to do what I wanted.

Money seemed to be very important, but I hated money, and I knew mom hated money because she never had any.

Could you imagine that mom made me save for two years so that I could buy a bike? I saved all the money I got from my birthdays and Christmas. Mom said, "If you wanted it, you would have to work for it." My friends all had bikes, and they did not have to work or save, they just got it. I asked my mom for a video game. Mom said that there was not enough money. She said I should start saving. I would be in my teens before I could have enough money to buy one. I put that video game dream out of my head because there was no way I was going to save for that.

At the park, mom always got the kids to jump rope and play games together. She would always say that this is the way to build a community, that this was the way to have fun, and it reminded her of St. Vincent. It builds community, and it's fun and reminds her of living in the old country of St.Vincent. Deep down, I knew mom just didn't want me to feel left out.

I tried to tell her things have changed and kids have games and fun gadgets now. Kids have their bikes, scooters, rollerblades hoverboards, and you name it my friends had it. It was about moving fast and having fun.

Mom said fun was not about money and having stuff. Mom said, "It's about enjoying the life and every moment. Talking to friends face to face, putting away electronics and living in the moment". Mom just did not get it, but I got it. I was going to help turn things around for us. I smiled in my head because this small boy knew what to do.

Today I was going to give mom a gift. It's not her birthday or anything like that, but I knew it was the right time to give her this gift. I knew It was the best gift ever and I made it all by myself. It was perfect! I knew it would help bring a smile to her face. Mom opened the gift looked at me with surprise in her eyes; She hugged me tightly and cried, sobbing uncontrollably.

This gift was supposed to make her happy, not cry, not get her upset and sad, that was not the plan I had. All I wanted was for her to be happy, to put a smile on her face.

Mom looked at me and said she was not upset, "but I asked why are you crying"? She said, "Actually I am happy, and sometimes happiness comes with tears."

She said, "I never knew you understood, you knew what was happening."

Mom was still uncertain and asked, "Why did you make me such a gift"? "How did you know a gift like this could help?"

I said." mom this superhero is for you. He was not just any superhero. He was made for children like me.

He was different; he fought poverty. He was going to help you, mom, and all other moms and their families that did not have enough. I didn't want other children to feel the way I felt. He was going to put a smile on children's faces."

I invented and drew him with all the gifts and talents that mom said were inside of me. I am still a little boy, but I knew what was happening around me. Don't forget children know and feel everything that's happening around them.

Mom held me tightly and cried and whispered **"Thank you for the gift, let's make our superhero a reality."**

Made in the USA
Columbia, SC
27 April 2019